CONNECT BIBLE STUDIES

TV Soaps

Telling Stories
Community Life
The Goings-on
Me and My Soaps

CONNECT BIBLE STUDIES: TV Soaps

Published in this format by Scripture Union, 207–209 Queensway, Bletchley, MK2 2EB, England.
Scripture Union is an international Christian charity working with churches in more than 130 countries providing resources to bring the good news about Jesus Christ to children, young people and families – and to encourage them to develop spiritually through the Bible and prayer. As well as a network of volunteers, staff and associates who run holidays, church-based events and school Christian groups, Scripture Union produces a wide range of publications and supports those who use the resources through training programmes.
Email: info@scriptureunion.org.uk
Internet: www.scriptureunion.org.uk

© Damaris Trust, PO Box 200, Southampton, SO17 2DL
Damaris Trust enables people to relate Christian faith and contemporary culture. It helps them to think about issues within society from a Christian perspective and explore God's truth as it is revealed in the Bible. Damaris provides resources via the Internet, workshops, publications and products.
Email: office@damaris.org
Internet: www.damaris.org

British Library Cataloguing-in-Publication Data: a catalogue record for this book is available from the British Library.
First published 2004 ISBN 1 84427 087 4
All rights reserved. Generally, any part of this publication may only be reproduced or transmitted in any form or by any means with prior permission of the copyright holder. But purchasers of this set of Connect Bible Studies may print, photocopy or otherwise reproduce the Members' Sheets for use in any group in which they are actively involved. In addition, the complete set may be printed or photocopied once for use in a single group.

ALSO AVAILABLE AS AN ELECTRONIC DOWNLOAD: www.connectbiblestudies.com

Damaris writers: Di Archer, Caroline Puntis, Tony Watkins
SU editors: Andrew Clark, Andrew Cupples

Cover design by Aricot Vert of Fleet, UK.

Cover photo © Granada Television. Used with permission.

Print production by CPO, Garcia Estate, Canterbury Road, Worthing, West Sussex, BN13 1BW.
CPO is a Christian publishing charity working in partnership with over 30,000 churches and other Christian organisations worldwide, using the power of design and print to convey the message of Jesus Christ. Established fro over 45 years, CPO is the UK's premier supplier of publicity and related resources to the UK Church, available through a direct mail catalogue series, an e-commerce website and most Christian bookshops.
Email: connect@cpo.org.uk
Internet: www.damaris.org/discuss/

Other titles in this series:

Harry Potter 1 85999 578 0	**TV Game Shows** 1 85999 609 4
Destiny's Child: *Survivor* 1 85999 613 2	**Lord of the Rings** 1 85999 634 5
The Simpsons 1 85999 529 2	**Dido:** *No Angel* 1 85999 679 5
Sven: *On Football* 1 85999 690 6	**Pullman:** *His Dark Materials* 1 85999 714 7
Friends 1 85999 775 9	**Madonna** 1 84427 032 7
James Bond 1 84427 007 6	**John Grisham's Thrillers** 1 84427 021 1
The Matrix Trilogy 1 824427 061 0	

Titles available as electronic download only:
U2: *All That You Can't Leave Behind/* **Billy Elliot/ Chocolat/ How to be Good/ AI: Artificial Intelligence/ Iris/ Superheroes**
And more titles following. Check www.connectbiblestudies.com for latest titles or ask at any good Christian bookshop.

Using Connect Bible Studies

What Are These Studies?

These innovative home group Bible studies have two aims. Firstly, to enable group members to dig into their Bibles and get to know them better. Secondly, by being based on contemporary films, books, TV programmes, music, etc., the aim is to help people think through topical issues in a biblical way.

It is not envisaged that all members will always be able to watch the films, play the music or read the books, or indeed that they will always want to. A summary is always provided. However, our vision is that knowing about these films and books empowers Christians to engage with friends and colleagues about them. Addressing issues from a biblical perspective gives Christians confidence that they know what they think, and can bring a distinctive angle to bear in conversations.

The studies are produced in sets of four – ie four weeks' worth of group Bible Study material. These are available in print published by Scripture Union from your local Christian bookshop, or via the Internet: www.connectbiblestudies.com. Anyone can sign up for a free monthly email newsletter that announces the new studies and provides other information (click on 'sign up' at www.connectbiblestudies.com).

How Do I Use Them?

These studies are designed to stimulate creative thought and discussion within a biblical context. Each section therefore has a range of questions or options from which you as leader may choose in order to tailor the study to your group's needs and desires. Different approaches may appeal at different times, so the studies aim to supply lots of choice. Whilst adhering to the main aim of corporate Bible study, some types of questions may enable this for your group better than others – so take your pick.

Group members should be supplied with the appropriate sheet that they can fill in, each one also showing the relevant summary.

Also from Scripture Union

church@home

SU's online magazine for the world of small groups

- ready-to-use sessions to try • inspirational articles
- 'how to' features • case studies on real groups
- reports of best practice • your space for your say
- info on training and resources

www.scriptureunion.org.uk/churchathome
the one-stop shop for all your small group needs

Also from Damaris Publishing

enables you to teach the message of the Bible in the language of contemporary popular culture

- Online database of quotes and illustrations from the latest films, music, TV etc
- Bible-briefings relating each Bible passage to relevant quotes and illustrations
- Complete youth group meeting plans
- Online master classes from expert speakers

www.talkstogo.com

Leader's notes contain:

1 Opening questions

These help your group settle in to discussion, while introducing the topics. They may be straightforward, personal or creative, but aim to provoke a response.

2 Summary

We suggest the summary of the book or film will follow now, read aloud if necessary. There may well be reactions that group members want to express even before getting on to the week's issue.

3 Key issue

Again, either read from the leader's notes, or summarise.

4 Bible study

Lots of choice here. Choose as appropriate to suit your group – get digging into the Bible. Background reading and texts for further help and study are suggested, but please use the material provided to inspire your group to explore their Bibles as much as possible. A concordance might be a handy standby for looking things up. A commentary could be useful too, such as the New Bible Commentary 21st century edition (IVP, 1994). The idea is to help people to engage with the truth of God's word, wrestling with it if necessary but making it their own.

Don't plan to work through every question here. Within each section the two questions explore roughly the same ground but from different angles or in different ways. Our advice is to take one question from each section. The questions are open-ended so each ought to yield good discussion – though of course any discussion in a Bible study may need prompting to go a little further.

5 Implications

Here the aim is to tie together the perspectives gained through Bible study and the impact of the book or film. The implications may be personal, a change in worldview, or new ideas for relating to non-churchgoers. Choose questions that adapt to the flow of the discussion.

6 Prayer

Leave time for it! We suggest a time of open prayer, or praying in pairs if the group would prefer. Encourage your members to focus on issues from your study that had a particular impact on them. Try different approaches to prayer – light a candle, say a prayer each, write prayers down, play quiet worship music – aiming to facilitate everyone to relate to God.

7 Background reading

You will find links to some background reading on the Connect Bible Studies website: www.connectbiblestudies.com

8 Online Discussion

You can discuss the studies online with others on the Connect Bible Studies website at www.damaris.org/discuss/

Scriptures referred to are taken from the Holy Bible, New International Version (NIV). Copyright © 1973, 1978, 1984 by International Bible Society. Other Bible translations can, of course, be used for the studies and having a range of translations in a group can be helpful and useful in discussion.

TV Soaps

Part One: Telling stories

Tracy: **Who's telling this story?**
Steve: **... that's all it is, a story!** (Coronation Street)

Please read Using Connect Bible Studies *(page 3) before leading a Bible study with this material.*

Opening Questions

Choose one of these questions.

Which is your favourite television soap opera and why?	What makes a good story?
Why do you think soaps are so popular?	Is watching soaps a good or a bad thing? Why?

Summary

The ability of soap operas to draw in millions of viewers every day has as much to do with the way the stories are told as with the stories themselves. In terms of dramatic tension and scenes of great emotion, soap stories never fail to deliver. We follow the characters' lives in bite-sized chunks, cutting from the resolution of one person's crisis to another character's trauma. For instance in *Neighbours*, just when Harold thinks he's sorted out all the problems concerning Lou's wedding to Trixie, the tables are turned and Harold suffers a stroke.

Everything about the soaps has a realistic bent – from storyline to set design. But this doesn't mean you'll never say, 'That would never happen in real life!' – the soap world is rather exaggerated realism. When gangland boss Andy Hunter takes an interest in EastEnders' Albert Square, he allows some things to pass but not others. He permits the notorious Den Watts, presumed dead for fourteen years, to slide back into the Square after his long exile. But when honest Shirley questions the way Andy runs his new betting shop, he fires her. There is always some form of help waiting in the wings, though – luckily for Shirley, the local punters are prepared to boycott the betting shop and join her protest.

As each episode draws to a close with an obligatory cliffhanger, the familiar theme tune starts up – *EastEnders* just wouldn't be the same without those drumbeats.

Key Issue: Telling stories

So how many soap operas do *you* watch? There's no getting away from the popularity of these everyday stories of everyday folk. Perhaps that sums up their appeal – they are based on realistic events with characters we can relate to. They are also cleverly designed to leave us in suspense, neatly picking up the threads in a subsequent episode. Loose ends are rare and the ongoing narratives invite us to tune in next time.

So what about the stories in the Bible? Are they composed of the same enticing stuff? How do biblical narratives – their characters and plot – compare to the world of soaps? In this study, we are looking at the way writers in the Bible tell their stories.

Bible Study

Choose one question from each section.

1 Realism

>Natalie: ***You can't change what's happened, can you? Or all the mistakes you've made?***
>Paul: ***But you can put it right though, can't you?***
>Natalie: ***Sometimes.*** (*EastEnders*)

- Read Genesis 37:1–11. Describe what is happening in this family. Which themes resonate with today's culture and why?

- Read Luke 10:25–37. How does Jesus grab the attention of his listeners? Which themes resonate with today's culture and why?

Leaders: The Samaritans were the descendants of Israel's northern tribes, who had intermarried with people from other nations. The Jews believed they had corrupted their faith, and resented the Samaritans building their own temple on Mount Gerizim. In 128 BC, the Jewish leader John Hyrcanus destroyed it. During Jesus' childhood, Samaritans desecrated the temple in Jerusalem by scattering bones, thus increasing the enmity (see John 4:9).

2 Crisis

>Shirley: ***Pat, do you know anything about employment law?***
>Pat: ***This is a caf' love, not an advice bureau!***
>Shirley: ***You sort of take it for granted, don't you, that you've got rights. I mean, you***

> *work hard ... And then a new owner comes along and that's you gone – without a second thought! Are you a member of a union? ... I wish I'd joined one now ... got some sort of back up, some protection.* (EastEnders)

Leaders: the passages in Section 3 follow on from the passages in Section 2 – the continuity is important so you should only look at Daniel 3 or Acts 12, not mix them up.

- ◆ Read Daniel 3:1–23. How does the tension build up through this story? What part do Shadrach, Meshach and Abednego play in bringing about the crisis?

- ◆ Read Acts 12:1–5. What factors set the scene for this crisis? How was the church involved?

3   Resolution

Shirley: ***What do we want?***
Crowd: ***Justice!***
Shirley: ***When do we want it?***
Crowd: ***Now!***
Andy: ***Not a particularly grown-up way to sort out our grievances, is it?***
Shirley: ***All I'm asking for is fair treatment, and I'm prepared to stay here until I get it.***
Andy: [Hands her an envelope.] ***A month's wages in lieu of notice. Not that I'm accepting liability, you understand. Just call it a gesture of goodwill.*** [Turns to crowd.] ***So, business as usual gents?*** (EastEnders)

- ◆ Read Daniel 3:24–30. How did God's resolution of this crisis affect Nebuchadnezzar? What makes this a good story?

- ◆ Read Acts 12:6–19. Why were Peter and the church astonished by God's resolution of this crisis? What makes this story so vivid? What were the consequences?

4   Ongoing narratives

Sharon: ***A postcard would've done ... Or a phone call.***
Den: ***It just wasn't possible.***
Sharon: ***I chose your coffin, I buried you, so anything's possible, isn't it?***
Den: ***I couldn't take the risk.***
Sharon: ***Oh please – you couldn't risk contacting your own daughter to tell her you weren't dead?*** (EastEnders)

- ◆ Read Exodus 6:6–8; Ezekiel 11:17–21; John 14:1–14; Revelation 21:1–8. What thread ties these verses together?

- ◆ Read Genesis 3:1–7; Genesis 6:5–8; Jeremiah 31:31–34; 1 John 3:1–6. Summarise this story in your own words.

Implications

Izzy: ***How can I tell him that the mother of his child is the same woman that broke up his parents' marriage?***
Will: ***This is a mess.***
Izzy: ***You have to tell him, Will.***
Will: ***No.***
Izzy: ***He deserves to know the truth, and he should hear it from you.*** (Hollyoaks)

Choose one or more of the following questions.

- What is the appeal of happy endings or endings where all the loose ends are tied up? How, as Christians, do we deal with life when it isn't like that?

- How would you show that the Bible is as relevant to your everyday life as soaps?

- How do you deal with crises in your life, or in the lives of others? How could your relationship with God be more in the centre of your responses?

- Do you have any unresolved crises in your life which need attention? How could your group help you?

- If the Bible and soaps demonstrate good storytelling, what could you learn about telling your own story of faith in Christ more effectively?

- How do you handle the fact that God doesn't guarantee to rescue us in every crisis?

- Do you believe that there is a big story, orchestrated by God, as described by the Bible? Discuss any problems you have with this.

Prayer

Spend some time praying through these issues.

Background Reading

You will find links to some background reading on the Connect Bible Studies website: www.damaris.org/cbs/eng/pg_background.html

Discuss

Discuss this study in the online discussion forums at www.damaris.org/discuss/

Members' Sheet: Telling Stories – Part 1

Summary

The ability of soap operas to draw in millions of viewers every day has as much to do with the way the stories are told as with the stories themselves. In terms of dramatic tension and scenes of great emotion, soap stories never fail to deliver. We follow the characters' lives in bite-sized chunks, cutting from the resolution of one person's crisis to another character's trauma. For instance in *Neighbours*, just when Harold thinks he's sorted out all the problems concerning Lou's wedding to Trixie, the tables are turned and Harold suffers a stroke.

Everything about the soaps has a realistic bent – from storyline to set design. But this doesn't mean you'll never say, 'That would never happen in real life!' – the soap world is rather exaggerated realism. When gangland boss Andy Hunter takes an interest in *EastEnders*' Albert Square, he allows some things to pass but not others. He permits the notorious Den Watts, presumed dead for fourteen years, to slide back into the Square after his long exile. But when honest Shirley questions the way Andy runs his new betting shop, he fires her. There is always some form of help waiting in the wings, though – luckily for Shirley, the local punters are prepared to boycott the betting shop and join her protest.

As each episode draws to a close with an obligatory cliffhanger, the familiar theme tune starts up – *EastEnders* just wouldn't be the same without those drumbeats.

Key Issue

Bible Study notes

Implications

Prayer

Discuss this study in the online discussion forums at www.connectbiblestudies.com

TV Soaps

Part Two: Community Life

Shirley: *If there's anything I can do to help in any way...* (*EastEnders*)

Please read Using Connect Bible Studies *(page 3) before leading a Bible study with this material.*

Opening Questions

Choose one of these questions.

Who is your favourite television soap character and why?	How realistic are the characters in soaps?
Is conflict inevitable in community? Why?	What are the best things about living in community? What are the hardest?

Summary

Ramsay Street has the Coffee Shop, Coronation Street has the Rovers Return, Albert Square has the Queen Vic, Emmerdale has the Woolpack – every soap community is built around the central location of a pub or a café. They provide places for the characters to meet, to fall out, to work alongside each another, to socialise together and to constantly gossip about the goings-on.

Like real communities, soap communities have their share of both good and bad relationships. When Dennis Watts, illegitimate son of Dirty Den, arrives in Albert Square, it looks like he is set to follow in his father's footsteps. Gradually, as the extent of his traumatic childhood is revealed, it becomes clear that all he needs to reform is the love of a good woman – enter Sharon Watts, Den's adopted daughter. But first, Dennis must help Sharon to get the upper hand in her feud with the Mitchell family, which goes back many years – and episodes.

Soap communities are places of great joy and deep despair. There's nothing like a soap wedding to bring out the best – and worst – in everyone. Steve McDonald's marriage to Karen looks set to go off without a hitch, despite the fiery nature of their relationship so far. But a surprise visit from Tracy ruins the day, when she turns up claiming that Steve is the real father of the baby she has just sold to the Croppers.

Key Issue: Community life

All TV soap operas are heavily community-based. We get to know the characters in one street or one village, and see their daily interactions. Strong personalities drive many of the plots, and friction between characters supplies much of the drama. How do they compare with the powerful personalities in the Bible? What does the Bible say about how people relate within communities? How can we celebrate the highs and lows of life with our neighbours, yet also deal with conflict when it arises?

Bible Study

Choose one question from each section. We suggest that you follow all the passages from Nehemiah, or all the passages about the church in Corinth.

1   Characters

Dennis: **Well, in this life you've got to look out for yourself, 'cos no one else is going to do it for you.**

Dot: **Don't I know it better than most. You know, you don't like people to know it, but deep down you've got a very good heart.**

Dennis: **Yeah, well, don't go spreading it around, eh?** (*EastEnders*)

- Read Nehemiah 1:1 – 2:10. What kind of a character was Nehemiah? How did Nehemiah's character shape these events?

   Leaders: During the Babylonian invasion of Israel, Jerusalem – including the temple and the walls – had been destroyed. It was decades later, after the exile, that Nehemiah led the process of rebuilding.

- Read Acts 18:1–18. What kind of characters does Paul come across in Corinth? What does the passage tell us about Paul's character?

   Leaders: Corinth was the commercial centre of southern Greece and had a very widespread reputation for immorality.

2   Neighbours

Lou: **We couldn't ask for a better bunch of friends and neighbours. We're going to miss you all. So until we see each other again, you all take care – be kind to each other.** (*Neighbours*)

- Read Nehemiah 2:11 – 3:16. How did Nehemiah get everyone involved? What does this account tell us about the builders?

- Read 1 Corinthians 10:23 – 11:1. What instructions does Paul give for being part of a community? What are the wider implications?

3 Conflict

Phil: *Sam, what you doing?*
Sam: *My job, what I get paid for. What's it look like?*
Phil: *... Do you know what this looks like? It looks like the Watts family say 'Jump!' and you, a Mitchell, say 'How high?' Is that your job, is it? Is that what you get paid for?* (EastEnders)

- Read Nehemiah 5:1–13. Why was this conflict a threat to the community? What principles did Nehemiah follow to sort things out?

Leaders: The economic crisis was compounded by wealthy people charging usury (high interest on loans) although the law prohibited this (see Exodus 22:25–27).

- Read 1 Corinthians 1:10–17; 6:1–8. In what ways did the Corinthians allow conflicts into their community? How does Paul challenge them and us?

4 Highs and lows

Karen: *You know what this wedding has made me realise? Just how much Steve must love me ... Yeah, all the money it's cost him, and the terrible time I've given him ... he's stuck with me. And he's done all this for me.*
Tracy: [Later, at Karen's and Steve's wedding.] *This is who the real father is – bridegroom Steve, not Roy Cropper ... Steve, that you're marrying, is the baby's father.*
Karen: *You lying little whore!*
Tracy: *Well then, why don't you ask him Karen? Go on.* (Coronation Street)

- Read Nehemiah 4:1–23; 6:15,16; 12:27–30. How did the 'highs and lows' affect the project and the people?

- Read 2 Corinthians 7:2–16. How does Paul account for troubles and joy – in his life and in the community? Why does he no longer have any regrets?

Implications

> Steve: *We can move away, get a new home.*
> Karen: *It isn't just where we live, Steve, it's where I work, it's where you've got your business.*
> Steve: *But together we could get through this, Karen. Together me and you can get through anything.* (Coronation Street)

Choose one or more of the following questions.

- Do you face problems in your local church/work/family community? What are the most important principles in resolving community conflict, and how can you apply them in your situation?

- How could you make more positive contributions to your local community?

- How could you support those who are trying to improve your community?

- What are the best ways of responding to people outside your community who are threatening it?

- Churches often fall out along doctrinal lines. Should those lines ever be drawn? Is unity or doctrine more important?

- How can we celebrate the good things more, especially within the Christian community? What would you like to do?

- What should the hallmarks of a thriving Christian community be? How could you help to make yours more like this?

Prayer
Spend some time praying through these issues.

Background Reading
You will find links to some background reading on the Connect Bible Studies website: www.damaris.org/cbs/eng/pg_background.html

Discuss
Discuss this study in the online discussion forums at www.damaris.org/discuss/

Members' Sheet – Part 2

Summary

Ramsay Street has the Coffee Shop, Coronation Street has the Rovers Return, Albert Square has the Queen Vic, Emmerdale has the Woolpack – every soap community is built around the central location of a pub or a café. They provide places for the characters to meet, to fall out, to work alongside each another, to socialise together and to constantly gossip about the goings-on.

Like real communities, soap communities have their share of both good and bad relationships. When Dennis Watts, illegitimate son of Dirty Den, arrives in Albert Square, it looks like he is set to follow in his father's footsteps. Gradually, as the extent of his traumatic childhood is revealed, it becomes clear that all he needs to reform is the love of a good woman – enter Sharon Watts, Den's adopted daughter. But first, Dennis must help Sharon to get the upper hand in her feud with the Mitchell family, which goes back many years – and episodes.

Soap communities are places of great joy and deep despair. There's nothing like a soap wedding to bring out the best – and worst – in everyone. Steve McDonald's marriage to Karen looks set to go off without a hitch, despite the fiery nature of their relationship so far. But a surprise visit from Tracy ruins the day, when she turns up claiming that Steve is the real father of the baby she has just sold to the Croppers.

Key Issue

Bible Study notes

Implications

Prayer

Discuss this study in the online discussion forums at www.connectbiblestudies.com

TV Soaps

Part Three: The goings-on

Edna: ***Kissing in the street at your age! Does the concept of dignity mean nothing to you?***
Pearl: ***No.***
Edna: ***In my day, there was a word for women of a certain age with inappropriate sleeping arrangements.***
Pearl: ***And what was that, Edna? Satisfied?*** (*Emmerdale*)

Please read Using Connect Bible Studies *(page 3) before leading a Bible study with this material.*

Opening Questions

Choose one of these questions.

Are the storylines in television soaps believable or not? Give examples.	Why is nothing ever straightforward in soap storylines?
What do you think about the treatment of moral issues in your favourite soap?	What are the most memorable goings-on in your favourite soap?

Summary

Storylines in soap operas twist and turn with remarkable agility. The interplay of relationships inevitably provides much of the drama. Soap operas always have one or two shady characters hanging around, causing mayhem – 'Dirty Den' in *EastEnders* inevitably springs to mind. At the other end of the spectrum, there is often a token Christian – Dot Cotton for example. In between are characters who get themselves and each other into all sorts of trouble – just because they're human.

Whether characters are loyal to each other or not is a key element in the soaps. For example, in *EastEnders*, because of the stress of his brother's illness, Adi cannot cope with newcomer Tariq and sees his family's acceptance of Tariq as a betrayal. Katie sleeps with her fiancé's brother the night before her wedding in *Emmerdale*; *Coronation Street's* Bev has a fling with Ciaran. Inevitably, these types of plots also raise questions of morality, with the issues varying from whether Janine murdered her husband in *EastEnders* to the involvement of Izzy in the collapse of Karl and Susan's marriage in *Neighbours*.

Many plots deliberately revolve around topical issues of the day. In *Neighbours*, Steph struggles with breast cancer and the Bishop family struggle with financial problems. *Emmerdale's* Donna has chlamydia, and may have started an outbreak in the village by sleeping with Robert; and in *Coronation Street*, Sarah's encounter with an online paedophile showed the dangers of internet chat rooms.

While the complicated plots often beggar belief, underneath most of the storylines lies the simple desire of the characters to be happy.

Key Issue: The goings-on

Family joys, sorrows and conflict; good and bad community interactions – these things are standard for soap storylines. Then there are the topical themes which reflect societal problems, like issues of race, terminal illness, justice or changing moral codes. So just how is the Bible relevant to the drama of our daily lives? In what ways does it help us with the underlying themes, like morality, loyalty or betrayal, upon which soap plots are based? How does it address the complications of life and relationships, or the over-riding pursuit of happiness which affects us all?

Bible Study

Choose one question from each section.

1 Morality

Robert: ***I want to stay here with you, be with you, sleep with you, wake up with you.***
Katie: ***Look, Donna could walk in on us at any minute, Robert.***
Robert: ***Well, we can lock the door.***
Katie: ***I'm getting married ... tomorrow!***
Robert: ***That's why I need to be with you ... tonight.*** (*Emmerdale*)

◆ Read 2 Samuel 13:1–22. What are the moral issues in this passage? What does this story tell us about the nature of sin?

Leaders: You may wish to follow Amnon's story in the next section.

◆ Read Luke 16:19–31. Why is the well-being of Lazarus a moral issue? Why would a warning to the rich man's brothers be useless?

2 Loyalty

Adi: ***Tariq's been 'investing' money from the stall ...***
Tariq: ***Look, I gave Vicky fifty quid to make us some sweatshirts. It's no big deal.***
Kareena: ***What's wrong with that?***
Adi: ***... It's the principle. He went behind my back!***
Ash: ***Come off it Adi, eh? Like Tariq says, it's no big deal. Anyway, isn't it Ronny we should be thinking about right now?*** (EastEnders)

◆ Read 2 Samuel 13:23–39. How does this story bring out both loyalty and betrayal in the characters?

◆ Read Acts 4:32 – 5:11. What was the motivation for being loyal in this community? Why do you think Ananias and Sapphira betrayed their community?

3 Complications

Susan: ***I can't keep going like this ... like I'm the only one who has any interest in making this marriage work.***
Karl: ***I have tried. I really have. But I feel suffocated when I'm with you ... it's like I'm two different people and I want to fight it, and make sense of it but I can't. Susan I – I am hating this. If I could snap my fingers and make it go away I would but I don't know how. I don't know how.*** (Neighbours)

◆ Read Judges 14:1–19. Describe the complications in Samson's relationships. How did they affect the outcome of this story?

◆ Read Acts 19:23 – 20:1. What were the complications of community life in Ephesus? How did the city clerk rescue the situation?

4 Pursuit of happiness

Karen: ***I wanted to be special. Just for one day – not the girl at the back of the class, or some face in a crowd, or a number on a clock-in card. I wanted to be the centre of attention, all eyes on me, everyone looking at me. Me, looking better than I've ever looked in my life.*** (Coronation Street)

◆ Read Genesis 29:10–30. What was Jacob's idea of happiness? What was it worth to him?

Leaders: After Jacob had tricked his brother Esau out of his birthright, Jacob fled to Laban, his uncle, in Paddam Aram.

◆ Read Matthew 6:25–34. What is the best thing we can pursue in our lives? Why are we tempted not to?

Implications

Steve: ***I'm sorry ... Look, I didn't choose for this to happen. She's ruined my day as well as yours!*** (Coronation Street)

Choose one or more of the following questions.

- What social justice issues are you passionate about? How could you do more to bring positive change?

- To feel betrayed is very hard. Do you have painful memories you need to let God heal?

- When do you find it hard to do the right thing rather than compromise? How could the group help you?

- What would you say to someone who thinks that 'sin' is an outdated concept and doing whatever you want is OK?

- What makes you really happy? Do you think God wants us to be happy? Why?

- Is there anything you have done to hurt others that needs sorting out with them or with God? Can you do it immediately?

- Do you think you make your life or relationships unnecessarily complicated? How could you live more simply? Could your group brainstorm ideas for this?

- Sometimes life can be too much like the constant drama of a soap. Is there anyone in your community who needs special support just now? How could you give it?

Prayer

Spend some time praying through these issues.

Background Reading

You will find links to some background reading on the Connect Bible Studies website: www.damaris.org/cbs/eng/pg_background.html

Discuss

Discuss this study in the online discussion forums at www.damaris.org/discuss/

Members' Sheet – Part 3

Summary

Storylines in soap operas twist and turn with remarkable agility. The interplay of relationships inevitably provides much of the drama. Soap operas always have one or two shady characters hanging around, causing mayhem – 'Dirty Den' in *EastEnders* inevitably springs to mind. At the other end of the spectrum, there is often a token Christian – Dot Cotton for example. In between are characters who get themselves and each other into all sorts of trouble – just because they're human.

Whether characters are loyal to each other or not is a key element in the soaps. For example, in *EastEnders*, because of the stress of his brother's illness, Adi cannot cope with newcomer Tariq and sees his family's acceptance of Tariq as a betrayal. Katie sleeps with her fiancé's brother the night before her wedding in *Emmerdale*; *Coronation Street's* Bev has a fling with Ciaran. Inevitably, these types of plots also raise questions of morality, with the issues varying from whether Janine murdered her husband in *EastEnders* to the involvement of Izzy in the collapse of Karl and Susan's marriage in *Neighbours*.

Many plots deliberately revolve around topical issues of the day. In *Neighbours*, Steph struggles with breast cancer and the Bishop family struggle with financial problems. *Emmerdale's* Donna has chlamydia, and may have started an outbreak in the village by sleeping with Robert; and in *Coronation Street*, Sarah's encounter with an online paedophile showed the dangers of internet chat rooms.

While the complicated plots often beggar belief, underneath most of the storylines lies the simple desire of the characters to be happy.

Key Issue

Bible Study notes

Implications

Prayer

Discuss this study in the online discussion forums at www.connectbiblestudies.com

TV Soaps

Part Four: Me and my soaps

Everybody's talking about it
BBC advert for *EastEnders*

Please read Using Connect Bible Studies *(page 3) before leading a Bible study with this material.*

Opening Questions

Choose one of these questions.

Are you hooked on a soap (go on, admit it!)? Why?	Do soaps influence your life at all? In what way?
Why do we discuss fictitious characters' actions? Why do we care?	What are the best and worst things about soaps?

Summary

Soap operas were first broadcast on American radio in the 1930s and targeted deliberately at housewives so that soap powder manufacturers could sponsor the programmes, hence the 'soap' label. But over the decades, soaps have gone mainstream, and now occupy a central role in television schedules. They've become a fixed part of the daily routine of many families. Soaps consistently command some of the highest viewing figures of any television programme. *Coronation Street* has only failed to make the annual list of top ten ITV programmes once since 1961. And Dirty Den's return to Albert Square attracted more than 16 million viewers in 2003, despite the rapid increase in the number of television channels splitting the audience in ever more directions.

For many people, the events which unfold in soaps day after day are hugely important. We feel like we share in the characters' lives. We talk about them at home and at work; we sit in judgement on their actions and motives; and we join in with their gossip.

Sometimes the boundary between fact and fiction gets very blurred. When Deirdre from *Coronation Street* was wrongfully imprisoned in 1998, the tabloid newspapers all joined the 'Free Deirdre' campaign. Tony Blair and William Hague even expressed their support. Although the campaign was the creation of a marketing company, the huge public support was a fascinating measure of just how much viewers engage with their soaps. This is what the programme-makers want, of course. They want us to identify with the ordinary characters, and return day after day to follow the various storylines as they weave in and out of each other.

Key Issue: Me and my soaps

Millions of us tune in every day to TV soaps, then go out and talk about the events and characters with our friends. We are invited to escape into make-believe worlds and care about what happens there. Is there anything wrong with this escapism? How does this compare with what the Bible wants to draw us into? What daily habits would the Bible recommend? What does it say about the way we are called upon to judge the goings-on in soaps? Finally, what does the Bible say about the influence that TV soap operas may have on us?

Bible Study

Choose one question from each section.

1 Engagement

[Soap operas work] because the audience has intimate familiarity with the characters and their lives. Through its characters the soap opera must connect with the experience of its audience, and its content must be stories of the ordinary. Dorothy Hobson, *Soap Opera* (Polity Press, 2002)

- Read Ezekiel 12:1–16. How did God use Ezekiel to engage with his people? What issues did he want to raise with them?

    Leaders: This prophecy was fulfilled in 586BC when a further wave of exiles was taken to Babylon, where Ezekiel was a prophet. Verses 12–16 refer to Zedekiah, installed as a puppet king in Jerusalem by the Babylonians. He attempted to escape from Jerusalem, but was caught and forced to watch his sons being slaughtered before being blinded himself.

- Read Luke 16:1–15. Why did this story engage Jesus' listeners? How did they react? Why?

    Leaders: Jesus told this parable to his disciples immediately after telling the parables of the lost sheep, lost coin and lost son to the Pharisees, rebuking them for their lack of concern for 'sinners'. Verse 14 makes clear that the Pharisees were still listening to Jesus.

2 Daily habit

Hi, If anyone has taped today's Hollyoaks omnibus I'd love to get hold of it – £10 + postage sound OK? Thanks. (*Hollyoaks* Internet discussion board)

- Read Daniel 6:1–14,21–23. How did Daniel's daily habit get him into and out of trouble?

- Read Psalm 119:161–176. Why is the Psalmist so keen to spend time with God? Describe the variety of ways in which he expresses himself to God?

3 Armchair judgements

Despite the twists and turns of the plot all our conclusions are essentially moral. Good triumphs, evil is punished and the value of human life is asserted. (John Yorke, former Executive Producer of *EastEnders*)

- Read 2 Samuel 12:1–14. How did David get from 'armchair judgement' to being right with God?

- Read Luke 7:36–50. What judgements did Simon the Pharisee make? How did Jesus turn them upside down?

4 Influence

In a fractured incoherent world, where community no longer means what it did, people hunger for drama and for universal truths that give them something to aspire to; something to make them feel better about humanity and about themselves. (John Yorke, former Executive Producer of *EastEnders*)

- Read Joshua 23:1–16. What dangers did Joshua see in the world around him? What choices did the Israelites have?

- Read Matthew 13:31–34; Mark 8:14–21. Why did Jesus talk about yeast to his disciples? Why are the disciples to welcome the influence of yeast in Matthew's account and watch out for it in Mark's?

Leaders: Yeast was forbidden in celebrating Passover and the Feast of Unleavened Bread which immediately followed it. Yeast wasn't used immediately before the escape from Egypt because of the need for haste. Yeast then came to represent impurity and was forbidden in any bread offered on the altar. However, it wasn't always thought to represent evil, as it was included in the firstfruits offering.

Implications

Most of all I love the fact that people want to watch stories that centre around one pivotal question – how do we, as citizens, in a bad and malevolent world, live a good life? How do we love? And most importantly what should we give up for others? (John Yorke, former Executive Producer of *EastEnders*)

Choose one or more of the following questions.

- Soap operas are full of characters that you are supposed to judge. Is this a good thing or a bad thing?

- Are you guilty of judging others in real life? What are you going to do about this?

- Do we identify with the extreme emotions being played out before our eyes in TV soaps? How can we make progress in dealing with our own tricky feelings?

- Does God come as number one in your longings and priorities? Why? How do you express this? Would you like it to change?

- What are the challenges you face in your world which could drag you away from God? How can you encourage yourself, and ask for support?

- Are there things in your lifestyle which do not reflect your relationship with God? What can you do about them?

- Where do you get your morals and values from? Which influences your thinking and behaviour most – TV or the Bible? Why?

- Are you going to change your TV soap viewing habits having done this study? Why/why not?

Prayer

Spend some time praying through these issues.

Background Reading

You will find links to some background reading on the Connect Bible Studies website: www.damaris.org/cbs/eng/pg_background.html

Discuss

Discuss this study in the online discussion forums at www.damaris.org/discuss/

Members' Sheet – Part 4

Summary

Soap operas were first broadcast on American radio in the 1930s and targeted deliberately at housewives so that soap powder manufacturers could sponsor the programmes, hence the 'soap' label. But over the decades, soaps have gone mainstream, and now occupy a central role in television schedules. They've become a fixed part of the daily routine of many families. Soaps consistently command some of the highest viewing figures of any television programme. *Coronation Street* has only failed to make the annual list of top ten ITV programmes once since 1961. And Dirty Den's return to Albert Square attracted more than 16 million viewers in 2003, despite the rapid increase in the number of television channels splitting the audience in ever more directions.

For many people, the events which unfold in soaps day after day are hugely important. We feel like we share in the characters' lives. We talk about them at home and at work; we sit in judgement on their actions and motives; and we join in with their gossip.

Sometimes the boundary between fact and fiction gets very blurred. When Deirdre from *Coronation Street* was wrongfully imprisoned in 1998, the tabloid newspapers all joined the 'Free Deirdre' campaign. Tony Blair and William Hague even expressed their support. Although the campaign was the creation of a marketing company, the huge public support was a fascinating measure of just how much viewers engage with their soaps. This is what the programme-makers want, of course. They want us to identify with the ordinary characters, and return day after day to follow the various storylines as they weave in and out of each other.

Key Issue

Bible Study notes

Implications

Prayer

Discuss this study in the online discussion forums at www.connectbiblestudies.com